Free Verse Editions

Edited by Jon Thompson

SPLIT THE CROW

SARAH SOUSA

Parlor Press
Anderson, South Carolina
www.parlorpress.com

Parlor Press LLC, Anderson, South Carolina, 29621

© 2015 by Parlor Press
All rights reserved.
Printed in the United States of America
S A N: 2 5 4 - 8 8 7 9

Library of Congress Cataloging-in-Publication Data

Sousa, Sarah.
  [Poems. Selections]
  Split the crow / Sarah Sousa.
      pages ; cm. -- (Free verse editions)
  ISBN 978-1-60235-635-1 (softcover : acid-free paper)
  I. Title.
  PS3619.O878A6 2015
  811'.6--dc23

                              2015002998

Cover design by David Blakesley
Cover art: "Fragments of Midnight" by Elise Mahan Used by
  permission.

Printed on acid-free paper.

                    1 2 3 4 5

Parlor Press, LLC is an independent publisher of scholarly and
trade titles in print and multimedia formats. This book is available
in paperback and ebook formats from Parlor Press on the World
Wide Web at http://www.parlorpress.com or through online and
brick-and-mortar bookstores. For submission information or to
find out about Parlor Press publications, write to Parlor Press,
3015 Brackenberry Drive, Anderson, South Carolina, 29621, or
email editor@parlorpress.com.

Contents

SPLIT THE CROW

I

Man's restless soul hath restless eyes and ears,
wanders in change of sorrows, cares and fears,
it faine would suck by the ears by the eye
something that might his hunger satisfy.

—Roger Williams, *A Key Into the Language of America*

I am not a man disguised as a crow.
I am night eating the sun.

—Michael Hannon *"What the Crow Said"*

Her Moods Caused Owls

To say the great horned
sits like a mask
in the tree. To say false face,

death mask, implies
I know the story.

The little snowy, light as powder
on a branch, is capable of cruelty
when her mood demands it:

ten torn crows turn up,
black feathers from bones.

To say the hollow bones were dead limbs
in a blow-down, sticks
strewn three miles wide, her moods
violent bursts, implies
I hold a story,

or that stories demand:
we want what is real
we want what it is real
don't deny us.

Once there was a girl who spoke
garlands; blossoms unspooled
from her mouth. Confused,
she tried to flee her own fecundity.
And her fear caused gardens.

I'm swallowing a story
that ends with blood-stained snow.
I know how this looks.
It appears to be true.

The Dead's Bright Copperas

Could it be held in a bottle like smoke
or liquor; the color of shadow. Could it
be one of the sad animals, one of the instinctual.
Sad because extinct but still
possessing mythical teeth, legs, claws.
Carnivorous and sad. Furred, plumed, spiny
and sad. Could it be hollow as the keeled sternum
of a gull or the pith of the cricket's flat
note. Could it be trapped like a song in the skull's
dull kettle. Sometimes resembling anemic condolence,
sometimes largesse. Primarily unique unless
born again of some woman. Could it be the sun
feasting wolf-like on the dead, its face set in bronze
by the dead's bright copperas. Could it be the sun
festoons the dead with necklaces and bracelets
of fat flies. Fishing for dead. Hunting the dead.
Always engaged in pursuits of the flesh.
Or could it be ghost infants who flop about
like trod-on birds. Without the strength to pass they stay;
eat our corn, settle invisible villages among us.
And wear their broken breastbones
like knocked-askew shields, stirring the flaps
of our doors—like a breeze their ingress and egress.

These Holes

We release the steam
            from heated stones.
How would thin spirits rise
otherwise; how could our ancestors wake
to whisper as we drowse?
            We have thresholds:
this riverbank, this fire. The first scoopful
of earth means we've entered it. A brother
will break the ground on my behalf one day
and slip me in:
my basswood mat a coracle.
When the son of Canonicus died
that chief burned his own palace down.
Threshold crossed.
            This sun at my neck was beaten
from a worn brass kettle. These holes
at my wrists the kettle sprung.

Trinket-Shine

at a Narragansett Indian Burial Site

This one was buried with a spoon held up to her face
so close her breath, if she breathed, would have fogged it.
This one was buried with her hands shielding a nose
decayed by syphilis. This other young woman
was buried without the usual adornment afforded young women.
Like tribal mothers, she took a few worn tools, a half moon
impressed on her hipbone, indicating full-term pregnancy.
Once she dreamed she was carrying, as a basket carries water,
three fetuses but only birthed a lame fawn
who wouldn't outgrow the dapple of snow
on its hind quarters. The graves lacking goods, as if robbed clean,
belong to children who suffered disfigurement:
spine bent like a scythe, unlinked and crumbling;
the enlarged head of hydrocephalus. No clear glass
beads strung on sinew, no rush bracelets
to tether their child-spirits. They had no names.
Had never been gifted with names.
In compensation, let their spirits wander.
Sometimes love is expressed with a stone
heavier than what lies beneath it. Best not hope
where both the crow and the corn are present.
God's black wing blots the trinket-shine.
This girl child *was* named, wore a delicate bracelet
made of yellow glass like grains.
Child who nearly lived, whose mother grew,
tended and harvested the corn, parched and ground
the corn, saved kernels for next spring's planting.
This daughter was wrapped in woven husk mats
and buried in a circular pit like a made gift—
small cake ready for the coals.

To Cure Foreboding Think of a Gray Horse

When sun shines through a downpour,
the devil is beating his wife. Slanting
rays draw from the sun's own deep well.

Beneath a mackerel sky the horse,
damp but unperturbed, crops the brown grass
low, hoofs strata of loam, sand, char,
quartzite, hematite, bone; scattered
tools disguised as rock. This bowl
scraper—the shoulder blade of a deer.
Think of a long village street
with fire pits in full flame, crackle
of fat and marrow. Excitement mounts.
That smudge in the distance
troubling you like an omen—
think of a gray horse.

Honey Out of the Rock

after Mary Rowlandson's captivity narrative

Foul is savory, water sweet. We glean
from fields trampled in the fighting:
sheaves of crickled wheat. I hide two ears
of corn beneath my apron.
Horse liver roasted over coals bleeds
bile on my tongue, horse's ears and feet,
ruff of small guts, cracked
and boiled bones, liquor of the bones,
maggots, dog and snake. My appetite
is wolfish. One day a deer is taken
with the fawn still inside her,
so tender—
I eat the soft bones as well as the flesh.

Body Interred With Fire-Making Tools

Flint and dry tinder,
a narrow bone tube to focus

the lungs' bellows on a single
spark, to magnify the breath in flame,

watch it lick the air, lap oxygen,
spread. Even in that mouthless

cave where nothing breathes,
a man might wake and crave

light, the companionship of shapes
on close walls. That the other

side may be womb-dark, a world in need
of creating. That *Man* necessitates *God*, splits

to play both roles, again
inventing fire. Inventing the means

for his survival
and his survival.

Roger Williams Among the Narragansett

During antler-shedding-moon I'm told
the mauquawwog, men-eaters,
prepare a monstrous delicious dish of brains.
They tell me all the tidbits
are used: ears, lips, eyes, the fat tongue.

I have wandered too long among this chaos
of ravens. I have a story too. I tell them
in God's swift blood-letting season
they will be the men.

Remove

after Mary Rowlandson's captivity narrative

Nine days on my knees. I leave
jelly-red bowls in the snow when I stand,
press crushed oak leaves to the wound
in my side as other captives suggest.
Remedies for the child are useless.
The bullet that grazed me lodged
deep inside that body. She moans
less. She slips as afternoon sun
slips down a wall and vanishes.

Making the Coracle

He enters the woods with a hatchet,
a pack basket and stones to strike sparks.
He fells a broad-trunked chestnut,
enters the tree with a hatchet.
He makes a small shelter with the bark of it;
sets fire and follows the burning with fire.
Steam from skin. Char-smooth
coracle hisses in the rain.
He exits the woods with a hatchet,
struck stones.

Of Creation

Man and woman were made of stone.
But Cautantowwit, displeased, broke them
into many pieces and the mica shone out
like stars. Our cut places still glimmer.

So he started over using trees.

Now you want the trees
to grow like corn, an inch for every rain.
You want the trees for ships—to take a gale,
rock on the angle, unbroken. You want the trees
to get you to another shore and back?
Better barter with the sea, god of tide-sucking
moon, god that rules your bird-caged lungs.
If the timbers of your roof stay true, thank the roof.

Remove

With morning I prepare to pick up my dead
and walk. The Indians bid me leave it,
lead me to my master's wigwam
where I sit alone. No one comes.
No comfort. Later I find they've buried her
on a hill in this wilderness.
Her name was Sarah. I say this
because she lacks a stone
and I'll never pass this way again.
Two Indians mounded the dirt
as though it must contain—in their fashion—
a handful of seed, a silver fish.

Body interred beneath a stone
slab pierced with a hole

so the soul can pass through
and *ushpeau* like smoke
                    or swift.

[Whippoorwill sings at the teetering
hours: darkness to dawn;
dusk into darkness. Hours that trick
like the firefly, because darkness
maybe does not reignite.]

That is our term for little child.

Grave of the Twelve-Year-Old Pequot Girl

1. Unearthing

Small as a tablespoon, her medicine
pouch holds the fragment of a psalm *sing
unto the lord a new song* and strands
of black European cloth, pseudomorphs
of paper and cloth: transformed to iron
salts where they touched an iron ladle.
We study the brittle bible, finger
the brittle cloth. The left forepaw of a bear,
nestled into the cave of her belly,
still sleeps there.

2. Interring

he hath done marvelous things the English
say, carry the little bound books at their hips,
the ant-letters' magic keeps them well
while whole tribes fall like grass at hard frost.
His right hand and his holy arm
(imagine the great arc of his holy arm)
hath gotten him the victory.
We gave her our strongest medicine.
We gave her their strongest medicine.

Of Hunger and Hospitality

If you stray fifty miles to the west,
the men will beat you to parched meal,
mix in fat and roast you in a copper kettle.
If death falls among *us,* we move
to fresh ground. Have you no trees?
Fire wanting? We're in a dearth ourselves,
no bone or tail. The wolf has robbed us.
Friend, for you I will divide in two
this last meat, dark
and sweet as a raven's wing.

Remove

They set fire to the wigwams and go

from wilderness through river and swamp
carrying all their trumpery with them:
old women on the backs of the young,
papoose wrapped tight as wooly larvae.

At first sign of the enemy,
corn, clearing and settlement
are abandoned. They push us on.

I watched the goodwife, heavy with child,
stop and have a game of ring-a-roses
played with hatchets on her skull.

Cold crossing, they push us through
dark water.
The captives who falter
fall deeper.

Snake, Fish, Stone

after the diary of Fidelia Fielding, Mohegan-Pequot

I saw a snake in the river
with a fish in his mouth,
swimming upstream like an eel;
head holding fish above water.
I should have hit the snake
with a stick but didn't have one.
I want fish to eat
but cannot catch one.

That stone is a house where witches gather
and make a fire inside to keep warm, maybe
eat a little bread and cheese. They rub
their hands by the fire, then divvy up the money.
That stone was so large yet disappeared.
Some around here say men destroyed it
in one great splintering.
And the witches were swept up
as rock dust, shards of silver.

I saw in the river a snake, he fixed me
with his poison eye. The fish flexed
like a muscle in the snake's mouth. I am hungry.
The snake is a cohort of witches.
If you ask, he *may* give you what you want.
More likely he'll give you what *he* wants.
Place him on the big stone and he'll whistle
like a stick being swung.

Body Interred With Mirror Ring

Sun on water, glass; sun on leaves,
looking-glass. Grave with slash of cardinal
flight, split bittersweet on snow, birth gore,
iron ore, ocher, clay. The rabbit
sparkles like a bowl of garnet beads; inside-
out. Oxidation coats everything. The rusted
kettle leaves red on your hands.
Send it down. Flesh, skin and bone
reduced to black smear in the bottom
of an empty hole. Each of us at the edge
embarks with the same weight: dead
memories, dead omens. Bells, beads and certain
keys, hammered brass and flint-spark:
send them down. Jewelry flashes
when the wearer is in motion;
when she stills start the mourning wail.
The earth opened once to take, releases
the long femur
from an overturned kettle: timpani,
sun on looking-glass, wail.

Narragansett Midwife's Testimony

Well, the law says I can't comply
when a woman, grown burly,
asks me for cramping herbs.
And I can't ignore weeping
breasts, her shift wet-through.
Clots in the chair she rises from betray her,
on the sheet where she passed
the night. The baby was found cold
and purple as a river stone. He lay
at the entrance to an Indian barn.
Not like an English barn, but a hole
in the earth where we bury things
we don't want stolen.

Incantation in a Jar, Sealed in a Tree

Beloved don't hate me
My heart is a rope you are braiding
don't be afraid
to tighten the strands
Moth Fire Choke Cherry
Beloved don't hate me
this rope that binds us won't break

Out of Wedlock

God took my heart for a stone, called me
his idea without hands. The baby came mottled.
I carried it hard, opened like a tributary
that last day. Do you know where it lies? No
one does. They would have hung me by the neck
for sure. When one dies, we lay down that name as dead.
But I *did* name him. He bore a broken
resemblance to his father,
light as a moth wing, light
as a moth at flame. Once delivered, still weak
in the thighs and stained, *that woman*
would have been dragged to her hanging place.
I have no name.

John Eliot Creates Indian Grammar

He lays together the *bones and ribs,*
takes what is quick and liquid
from their tongues. Pins
their *ululations* to parchment.
The first bible printed in the new
world is Algonquin—European
funded. Bible indecipherable to Europeans
and tribes
of the Algonquin.

He begins with a foundation: verb substantive,
indicative, imperative and optative modes.
He places the bones:

I am white
thou art white.
my whiteness
thy whiteness

thou are kept
he is kept
we are kept
I wish thou be kept. He wishes

them to know, the language of the bible is
the language of bondage, all men possessed

before tongues. He wishes them
to know *cleave* is both
cut and *cling to.*

Judges

bricolage from the bible marginalia of Massachusett Indians

I am not able to defend myself
from the happenings in this world.

I Job
I Joseph

God is just and good,
also you can receive him a second
time in heaven.

I am a person.
I am pitiful.

Nothing is evil in what he says
this god who is in heaven.

Many have read
this book
to hear his commandment

to be commanded.

You, my friends
who are of the world,

should remember:

the spirit your spirits are with
is sinful. We know nothing

of this world, this land.

We have eaten it all
I and my children,
we have used it all
my children and I.

Only God's leaf shall not wither.

I, Joseph
(God's leaf shall not wither)

I am a man.

Dear Reverend,

I believe Satan wishes to partner me
in dance, split my sums, confuse my English.
When I bleed, Satan sticks his finger in
the hole and paints a hunting scene on skin.
I pray. I try to concentrate. Satan says
I talk above my head. I believe Satan
switches my tea for stronger drink, makes me think
of mountains' purple crowns on winter mornings
when I should be here on the hard bench.
Satan makes me homesick for tender
pearls of corn, makes me fantasize sweet
milk in the throat. Satan whispers like the sea,
a flock of wings. Satan makes me desire flesh:
of fish, foul and beast, my own flesh unencumbered
for hard dancing; moon-of-the-sage-hen's-
dancing. Satan leads me down
onto a bed of skins and earth:
my skin, my earth.
He reminds me that I like this.
Reverend, I believe Satan is easier
with me than with anyone else in the world.

Body Interred with a Fishhook

'Fisher of men' means god
who walks on waves,
proffers bread and wine as lure;
means the men who take our land and mete
it out like pinched crumbs.

This hook's not embedded
in flesh—barbed, eyeless, made of brass,
with a nick to secure the bast string
and a copper tube holding coiled line
in case he needs to feed
out more. See, the fish leads chase,
the length of which the fisher determines.

Deer Island

Plovers nest where sand meets the bones
of rose thorn and beach plum, sigh
of dry cordgrass, of paspalum.

Where sand meets rose thorn, coyotes
slip the beach plum fence.
Winter wind whips up waves,

scours the sand for nests, and daylight
drains from the east. Come the calls
of Sora and Whippoorwill. That fistful

of feathers the black rail sings
take my light, sings coyotes from
their rose thorn cover

to pilfer every nest. Coyotes whine
hoarse as cordgrass as paspalum; the light
drains from plover nests upshore.

Come sinew cry, coyote whine
mingled in a single throat.

Passage

after the diary of Fidelia Fielding

Cold for one alone.
The wind goes past, whistling.
Sun is up, it is noon, the sun goes down.
Day hurries away and no one
can get ahead. I cannot
make a tree, add one leaf
or feather the wind.
The sun is gone, day gone
dusky. Already it is night.
There is a fox, and a hound following.
Snow falling toward night.

II

Provenance

The placard says
this twine-woven basket
was not found

in any grave. The basket is
behind museum glass;
its story complete

on white cardstock.
An Indian woman wove it
as payment for a sip of milk

offered by the major's wife.
By the river she sat, unraveled
an edge of her blanket, peeled

the inner bark from a wickup tree
and wove in a piece of dry husk,
which rattled like a price tag in the breeze.

She made a small nest, the story says,
and would have dropped a warm egg
into the nest herself before she presented it

to the major's wife. She was that grateful,
kindness that rare. The placard says
the basket's coiled and scarlet

statement is safe behind glass
due to that major's wife. The path
this trickle of red threads through the weft,

a monologue, almost
contemporary. *Dead language*
the placard says.

Removal

Treaty of Dancing Rabbit Creek

Give us your thimbles and thread.
Give us the rosaries worn
at your necks, your hatchets
and hammers. Give us your knives
and your forks, the broken ones too.
Give us your pitchers and pans,
spoons and brass kettles. Give us your hoes, bell
collars, bridles. Give us your plows
and your colts, your fertile creek
bottoms. Give us the corn that is coming along,
tight as the ears of a squirrel. Give us your trees.
We've made other arrangements.
Give us your tired and scared
but leave the table and the chairs.
Give us your cabins, your two-story houses.
What does an Indian need with two stories?
Give us your guns and your shot.
Sign your names, your symbols or marks.
Brothers, give up your numbers; let us enumerate.
We've set fire to your cabins and crops,
our plows have found your people's graves.
We've made other arrangements:
just over the river, four-hundred miles
west, land is waiting; for each family a blanket.

Loss

after Pretty-Shield

Our hearts were light as breath-feathers.

Drums and dancing, flames
like tongues licking a yellow bone.

All about the fire, one could see how much a man
loved his woman by her softly braided hair, his

gentle fingers at her neck. Smoke rose
and rode the wind. *The drums and the dancing*

stopped—
        a lodge
fire doused with a kettle of water.

My heart dropped like a kicking-ball
stuffed with wiry hair. We fasted.

Moon of the sage-hen's dancing
came and went without dancing.

I carried the rusted gun in my chest.

Moon of the ripening berries
came without feast.

We were nearly starved from our sorrow,
traces of blood still in the hollows

of our women's cheeks. Their own claw
marks fading from their necks.

Incantation to Affect Two Women

loneliness itself will be breaking your two souls along the valley

Now, little white dog

I have come to fondle your soul

The mourning doves call

you purchased her soul

Like a field-clod, like a dead crow

I turn over your soul

The whippoorwill knows

I perch on your soul,

white shadow,

drained soul.

I've come to rattle

the pebble in your soul

I make the fire rise to its feet,

like smoke I pass through your soul.

Your heart spits in the flames
put the black fork in my hand.

Courtship scene drawn on an envelope

over the address of Commanding Officer
Second Cavalry, whose presence fails
to chaperone the lovers—slipping
from their separate tipis, blankets damp
with morning. The creek's wavy line
in mizzle-light is edged with shrubs
like small fires. The lovers share a blanket.
Beneath the hem, feet,
multiplied to indicate haste from tipi
to courting place. In one torn corner,
removed from his narrow waist
a feathered dagger
like a flame inching up the page,
the empty water bucket she thought to bring.

Contrition

from the Latin 'ground to pieces'

> *"With the first offence, adulterers lost their ears, with the second,*
> *their noses and upper lips and with the third, their lives"*
>
> —Adair's *History of the North American Indians*

You come to me faceless, possibly dead.
We say dreams are just the mind warming
to the day's events. We say dreams are prophecy,
revenge fantasy. The first night, you arrive
holding your own pale ears in your palm
like pressed sugar, strange wafers.
The second night your nose is gone:
two ugly holes
are flush with your face like a snake's.
On the third night, your lovely
lips have been shaved
off. You seem to plead; my throat
is tight from not responding. Her face
I took care of all at once. I was surprised
to find my hands gripped onto her ears
as onto the small handles of a vase.
It's easy to break something so breakable
as it must be easy to seduce the willing,
against that tree, again and again against that rock.
It would have been harder *not* to break her
unrepentant face. That's how I know *you*
were contrite: your face fell off and then you died.

Removal

It is said the women wended
their way in the dark between empty
cabins, cold fire pits, into the forest
they would abandon. It is said the procession
was formal. They wore embroidered robes
similar to the ones the Hopi lay
upon the ground when the first horses
entered their country. Sacred horses.
Sacred trees. It is said the women whispered
to oaks and elms, wept and stroked
the bark as a mother strokes her child,
one last lull,
      sleep.

She makes a ghost of herself then
leaves leaves leaves.

The Art of Flying

Apply intent like gentle pressure
to a wound. Superfluous maybe,
but the arms should be extended.
First, a height scaled, a precipice
achieved. Read: a jumping off
place. Let go, get heavy
as when you pass from this world
to the other nightly. Breach the flimsy wall.
To rise up, you must sink
like a tonnage of links. Recognize
your intent, but obliquely,
through a half-closed eye. Bow to gravity
as the noose you'll be slipping.
To join the hollow boned you'll have
to cast your body down, cast it off
like a wedge of sunlight sliding
from the wall, like the fly
giving its husk to a hook and a nylon line.
But you're not tethered and you're not
weightless. So plummet.
Invest not in flight, but falling.
The most you can do is believe
air is measured in fathoms
and bottomless, that earth is a myth
created by birds who would kill for a rest.

Doomed of Oklahoma

Nowhere to stretch your heart

If Noah's Ark was a ship intended to sink
with its freight, and all the animals,
two by two, had been duped
into thinking they were getting the deal,
when really the ark was an expedient
way to dispose of riff raff and half breeds,
peculiar species. If Noah and his wife were squatting
with guns in your bunk, ready to jump
your claim, and all the two by twos were clashing
horns, claws, teeth in the dwindling space.
And the ark moaned, riding low in the waves
of Oklahoma. If the Ark was babel and doomed

Issue Days

The women brought ponies
to carry home the issued meat.

Once the clerk stamped a ration ticket
the beef would be released,

hoofing and panicked, into a larger corral.
Each head of household, like a warrior

painted and regaled, came forward
goading his horse to the hunt.

The beef were almost as wild, *almost*
as unpredictable as buffalo.

When the animal was shot,
the women moved in with knives.

Each got a piece of warm liver or heart
before the long trek home

and real feasting; lodge walls and
skin doors propped open.

Smoke from our fires diminished the sun.

They put an end to the hunt
on issue days: *to shorten the process*.

After this our meat was cut for us.

Molly became Cherokee

because a man named Dent beat his first wife
and the baby, hard as a moon in her belly.
Because he beat them dead,
this white man purchased a slave named Molly
and gave her to his wife's kin, the Deer Clan.
Because the women took Molly as a sister,
made her Cherokee. Because she had a son
of a Cherokee who didn't beat or rape her.
Because Dent had sold Molly on paper
before he gave her to the deer clan,
a white family came and claimed mother and son.
Because the deer clan fought them
in court to keep their hands off this Cherokee.
Because Dent kept his hard fists off this one.
Because she was not his property
or their property or any property
now. She was a gift given.

Removal

Broken-foot-trail. Trail of small bones picked clean.
Winter when the children died of coughing.
Infested blankets. Moon of the popping trees. Coughing.
One blanket, two blanket. Trail of blackened feet.
Ghost limbs. Crying. She of sinew and awl.
He of knife and bow. People who walk.
Walk-until-falling. Trail to the deer's watering hole.
Dysentery. Winter when our bones creaked like trees.
Coughing. Hatchet at the throat
of the tree. Rock mounds. People of kicked hearts.
People who walk. Walk until falling.
Dysentery. Coughing. Winter of bark-eaters.
Winter of lichen. People who carry seeds.
Winter of snapped bones. Frostbite.
People of snow blindness.

Turning

We thought doors and windows were carved into houses
so we could watch white people
doing their work, speaking their language.
When we cut off our braids and put on
gray cloth, we began to look out
from *inside*— our own trees like sticks in rows,
our own breach-easy fences.
Once we divided a day by the sun's rising,
apex and setting, weeks by sleeps.
We dealt in halves and quarters. But we learned
soon enough to consult the white face
before eating and sleeping.
We learned that day may be broken
further, into splint-thin shavings. How the civilized
man must account for these units.
One squandered second creates a gap—
and the ticking of rain on leaves stretches to fill it.
Once squandered never retrieved. We learned
to turn furrows in our sleep, bone deep.
We trained the harnessed war-horse to turn
his anger under, turn it under.

These Holes

To rasp willow splints for baskets,
draw strips through the eye
in the hip bone of a deer
over and over
until the green willow splint
is soft as hair.

Trained doctors amputated and debrided
bone. Cherokee doctors treated the lesser
wounds, soaked strips of slippery elm
in cold water until pliable, then passed the strips
through bullet holes, especially in the chest.
Dirt, blood clots, bits of bone
from other men, stuck to the elm's mucilage. The pieces
were drawn like cloth run through the eye
of a gun, until the open wound was clean
as flesh can be, as the watery eye of an unsealed oyster.
Maybe the doctors' faces hovered low and intimate
over their patients. Maybe they applied pressure,
packed the holes with more herbs, said some words.
Maybe the words were those of the Indian
in that Jarmusch movie, gouging the bullet
from the outlaw's chest with knife and fingers
chanting a little, muttering: *stupid fucking white man.*

Peculiar Confederacy

You turn our bones up
beneath your plows, ghost the trees.
Our shadows barely reach your knees.
We hike through swamp
to retrieve your slaves. Call us
sharpshooter, scout, medicine man.
We cut to the thigh to save the leg. So
how do you like your Indian now? Say how
white we have become, how American.

Man Sharpening a Scythe

Creates a wishbone
shape. Blur
of blade questioning
                blade. Hand and
        handle hold
                        the scene
in stasis. A wish
            bone's width between
handle and blade.
                Milkweed down,
broken heads and chaff.
                    The pastoral scene
blinks,
            reality hits bone:

            a chaos of wings.
Blade, hand, blade.

Another crow hangs

from a stick in the cornfield.
Another farmer employs the law
of reverse attraction. Repulsion requires
a little oily blood draining from the beak,
the sleek body snagged in flight,
gone slack as a scare. No crow
rescue party circles, no lone mate
hobbles around the base of the stick,
willing to be martyred.
Crows fly with their landing gear down.
Not sky, but ground is their true habitat—
a sharp, lineated cornfield; crosshatched
as a lover's missive. What she burned
to say she fever-scratched *you saw*
a bullet hit
a bird and he told you
he wasn't shot-
And you believed

what you wanted to believe.

Deed of Gift

None would eat the flesh
cooked by a Cherokee woman with child
or follow the path she traveled,
so fearful her power.
But a coal black slave carrying low
the property of an Indian?
Not a cruel man but fond of whiskey
and gambling. The deed, drawn up
while he was drunk on lust
for the trader's daughter, specified:
silk scarves, one slave woman
and her unborn, three pistols.
A Cherokee child belonged to his mother's
clan. Her own line died inside the rank belly
of a ship carrying livestock, her line severed like a neck
on the auction block. The women warned her
off speckled trout: it would mottle the baby;
kept her from strawberries to avoid the stain.
But their care knew portions. All would eat her
corn mash with venison. Even when her belly bulged over the pots,
they called her master's table fine. Like white folks
none offered to sing her baby home.

Indian Exhibit; The Trans-Mississippi and International Exhibition 1898

The Indian band strikes up Stars and Stripes Forever—
familiar distress signal of circus performers everywhere.
Down the midway waving *scalps* cut from cowhide.
The Improved Order of Red Men play friendly
Indians to the white man's clever cowboy. The sham
battle; a march to the reservation. Wander through the living
diorama, open day and night: this is how they cook
on open fire, this is how they cry.
Three Indians die and one attempts suicide
behind the scenes. *This grass house and tipi and windbreak;*
the only authentic artifacts says the ethnologist
James Mooney on arrival from Oklahoma
with 106 authentic Kiowa and their ponies.
He carries his grass house like a social studies project.
This lead buffalo, these miniature Indians
holding twigs for arrows. Real sized Indians
brandishing blanks. *See*

these once formidable enemies
of white man
camped together in a frame—

Renaming at Boarding School

Dawn-of-Day became *john rogers,*
Pretty Deer chose *caroline,*
Littlecreek to *johnson*
Raincloud dulled to *brown.*
Iron Hawk and Everywind bound themselves
to walk with mules and milk the cows.
Teacher offers names of white
people. Turtle becomes *tuttle*
smith will work for
Sitting. No one is named
Stately, try *stanley.* Redeagle/*edmunds,*
Whitefeather/*whitaker,* Omen/
amen. Teacher erases names,
the names which shame and startle:
Blowsnake, Greet-the-Spear,
Puts-On-Shoes, Runs-Away-From-Here.

The Lost People

Stony Indians of Canada
called the young people who had
been taken away to boarding schools
ainstikn ustombe, 'the lost people'

Influenza came like spirits in the night;
steam whistle in my ears,
pistons pounding. Influenza's fingers
danced over my body like *feathers on sore spots.*
Hair shaved to the skull again. The first time;
hundreds of braids severed and tossed onto the fire
like smudge, along with the little medicine
bags our mothers packed. We were given new
ceremonies. *Learning to Sweep*
reads the photo of young boys lined up with brooms
taller than themselves. *Pilgrims and Indians*:
all the parts played by Indians. I know
influenza is a white man's disease
because it cuffs me upside the head when I think
in Sioux, though the hospital is named *wayazanka tipi*
and the library is *Wowapiopahi,*
(pile of books). When a boy emerges
from wayazanka beneath a sheet, they carve
his tribe like a surname into the stone
above him: Creek, Menominee, Kiowa, Sioux.
Tuberculosis, pneumonia, influenza took
some. Speaking Kiowa could get a boy thrown
across the room, collar bone snapped like a bird who flew
against a wall. On the train coming east,
not knowing what else to do, boys sang
the death songs our warriors sang riding into battle.

Survival and Other Skills

A girl marks how close to the stick her marble rolls
or if it touches. Girls learn patience young.
All our people learn to detect subtlety,
track the movement of a distant object between
two sage twigs screwed into dirt. The dot
makes slow progress from pole to pole.
Dot becomes buffalo, horse, man.

At ten years old each girl is given a kit containing
knives, awls, sinew, needles. During village raids,
a woman would snatch up her kit
along with her children. With these few tools
tribes could begin again: tipis, moccasins,
drinking skins, robes.

When our girls were taken they left
their tools behind. Six, sometimes seven years
before they returned, unable to speak
with their own grandmothers. But they could sweep
a kitchen fine, cut hair, make light biscuits.
And they could *embroider*.
Each brought home a few hanks
of thread— barely enough for flowers

Scrapbook of the Anonymous Lace Maker

The Population Report; 1861 peeks from pasted,
yellowed squares of newsprint; *corner fan wheel lace*
strong arms *wheelwrights: 58.* Her handwritten treatment
for diphtheria, for scarlet fever:
mix sulphur with sugar to make it palatable,
challenges the introduction by Hiram Stevens M.D
who bemoans population loss due to westward drift.
Nineteen cases of suicide didn't help, at least
two by *cut-throat,* two by *otherwise. Not stated.*
Of violent deaths, drowning topped the list,
followed by burns and scalds and railroad accidents.
What to make of *border for table cover* concealing
the numbers for *polypus in nose, scarletina and scorbutus?*
The lace maker is busy pasting
cross-stitch for *darned tidy.* Her subtle plan
to order the messy enterprise of love, procreation
and dying with a pair of sharp scissors
and a glue pot. Why then does she leave the table-
of-contents page for diseases bare, so: *how to shade*
a braided mat must face *dropsy;* out of its league
against even *conventional diseases* like *apoplexy,*
as well as the *local diseases.* Though *bronchitis*
sounds almost homey. Come the litany of *stillbirths,*
scalds and poisonings, she turns the page and annotates
the table: *births and marriages* with a clear handwritten recipe:
100 pounds of pickle for pork or beef. Beside the open-worked
pattern for *turret edged lace* read *debility......*
marasmus...... A breakdown of the sexes
by town faces *What Constitutes a Perfectly Sanitary House.*
But when we arrive at the clipping: *How to Kill Quack Grass*
we begin to suspect her interests
as diversions. And when we find *a child's crocheted hood*
coyly placed beside the grid showing births
for *Cavendish* through *Woodstock,* we know
the next page will bring, like a good neighbor to a potluck:
stewed pears, pickled eggs, whooping cough.

The Pan-American Exhibition; Buffalo 1901

Tuberculosis hits the Filipino Village hard.
Eight advanced cases
in the Indian Congress, eleven of measles
at Eskimo Camp and three
of fatal pneumonia.

Behold, the world
is a sucked orange

After the quarantine is lifted, observe
the plains' Indian contemplate
a wolf. Like old friends meeting
after many trials, see the recognition
pass between them. When one howls,
the other is tempted.

The Myth of Fish

Each man dug up four of the root
called *devil's shoestring*, long and
smooth like a worm. He smashed
the roots to pulp with stones,
and the greenish stringy pith bled white.

It is said they dammed the stream
with poles at both ends and the roots
were set to soak until the creek turned cloudy.

Not poisoned exactly, but those fish were knocked
unconscious until dozens floated, pale belly, to the surface
like something you wouldn't want to eat.
Families gathered them like acorns.

The larger fish were only dazed
so the boys had good sport shooting them
with light arrows. They did this in little

creeks here and there, removed
the pole dams to let the water run clear.
But the government found out and put a stop to it.

* *

Trace amounts of anti anxiety
drugs were found in wild perch this century.

So scientists tainted man-made ponds
with the same drugs—

Before Oxazepam perch were shy.
Afterward they became bold and antisocial.

They wanted to swim on their own.
Some even avoided schools as much as possible.

Fluoxetine and Estradiol lowered the inhibitions
of fathead minnow. Ibuprofin reduced the libido
of male zebra fish.

In the wild, drugged fish became
fish in a barrel: 24/7
risk-takers. Lost the instinct to swarm or scatter
when a shadow swept over,
when beak or bullet broke the surface.

* *

Now that we don't eat fish, we catch them by hand.
Our wriggling fingers remind them of worms.
The fish latch-on to pinkies and suck
like babies once did. We used to kiss
and throw back the small and the bad ones,
for favor:

*We offer this to you who are down
in the water with wings of red,* that sort of thing.

Now every fish is foul—
yellow, liver spotted, brackish.
We kiss them black and blue.

Flea Market

Remember when all the trees were up
for sale, marked with ribbons?
The ribbons said: cut
this tree, take this one.

A hundred price tags shake
like leaves in the wind,
in the breeze of an oscillating fan,
a dirty skiff the open door let in.
Price tags in a wind like
white leaves on strings.

Remember when
all the trees are sold became
just more words we spoke.

Monsanto kills the bees

for cross-pollinating. After suing the farmers,
they gag the wind. The next generation

of seed achieves sterility. Prepare the pigweed soup.
Or we'll learn to eat like shrikes: meet the carrion
rose. Consider the Lilies®:

blight-resistant, aphid-repelling; each flower's thousand
corms edible for an hour. Quadruple trumpeted
beauty surpassed only by their industry. Behold
American ingenuity. How we toil.
How we spin and spin and spin.

Sometimes They Keep a Horse

Sometimes they keep a horse in the pen,
a stout horse beside his batten shed.
Some days that plot is empty,
fence posts stand like bitten fingers.

A stout horse beside his sway-backed shed—
the daughter's horse, daughter's gone;
fence posts like missing fingers.
Comes the man from town with soothing sounds and rope.

The daughter's horse. Daughter's gone.
A clothesline flaps with clipped wings,
whisperings and rope.
Sometimes they keep a horse beside the roses.

The clothesline flaps with clipped wings
out of a painting in lime and ocher.
See the horse? See the roses?
No. That plot is empty.

Split the Crow

and you'll find two men inside
a canoe playing a hand saw or is it a band
saw, another building an out-of-tune fiddle.
Snake rattle, corn blade. It's dark in there
you'll find. A continent, a well-provisioned
burial hole: coins, green vitriol, damaged
remains. And you'll find human
grease feeding the flames. Corvine
caw feral as a fox, wide as a grave. Song that sucks
the air out. Mourning doves calling
gule' hu. who. Ghosts touching
gasoline to their tongues. Ghosts
auroral. And you'll find sadness
like maggots riddles the flesh,
makes the chest rise and fall, a simulacrum
you're willing to swallow. Bones buried
deep in the tilth as if planted to grow.
Heart like a sleeping-bean, the wing bones'
swift crockery. Twelve ounces
is common enough: odorless, colorless;
encased in iron, would it melt
in a fire? You'll find you're fine with one
crow, two, three crows torn
for you; crows for stewing and feather-strewing.
You'll find it's *you* who split
the crow and didn't stop there
but entered the crow with a fork
and pulled the crow shut behind you.

Notes

I

Her Moods Caused Owls

The phrase was adapted from the line in a Swampy Cree story *It was also known his moods caused various owls.*
We want what is real/we want what is real/Don't deny us was adapted from a Crow song.
The Language of the Birds edited by David M. Guss

Honey Out of the Rock

In February 1675, Mary Rowlandson, the wife of a minister away in Boston, was taken from her home in the central Massachusetts town of Lancaster during a bloody raid by a coalition of Nipmuc, Narragansett and Wampanoag Indians led by Metacom, also referred to as King Philip. The raid signaled the beginning of King Philip's War, which took the lives of about five thousand Native Americans and two thousand five hundred European settlers. Rowlandson, along with family and neighbors, was marched for eleven weeks and five days, about 137 miles, through western and northern Massachusetts into southern Vermont and nearly back to Lancaster where she was "redeemed" or ransomed to her family. Six years after her ordeal, Rowlandson wrote and published her story, titled: *The Sovereignty and Goodness of God,* in which she invested a Job-like spiritual trial to her experience. Ironically, the typesetter of Rowlandson's book was a Native American printer's apprentice who had also been held captive by Metacom's coalition and forced to fight.

eat the bones as well as the flesh was taken from *The Sovereignty and Goodness of God* by Mary Rowlandson

Body Interred With Fire-Making Tools

Some characteristics of burial goods in this poem and the other interment poems can be found in the books *Cautantowwit's House: An Indian Burial Ground on the Island of Conanicut in Narragansett Bay* by William Scranton Simmons and *Burr's Hill: A 17ᵗʰ Century*

Wampanoag Burial Ground in Warren, Rhode Island edited by Susan
G. Gibson

Roger Williams Among the Narragansett
Roger Williams lived peaceably among, and was at times sheltered
by, the Narragansett Tribe of Rhode Island after his banishment
from the Massachusetts Bay Colony. On several occasions he ad-
vocated on the tribe's behalf with Bay Colony officials who seemed
eager for conflict. However, Williams' was also a Christian of his
time, in that he believed the Indians to be heathens, spiritually
lost and even damned. In his cultural treatise on the Narragansett
Tribe *A Key Into the Language of America* he referred to all Indians as
"wolves with men's minds" and their living quarters as "dirty, stink-
ing smoke holes".

Remove
Rowlandson ordered her captivity narrative into "Removes", each
section signifying the group's removal from a location where they
rested or passed the night. There were twenty removes.

Of Creation
Cautantowwit was the Narragansett God of the southwest, whose
house souls traveled to after death.
In his *A Key Into the Language of America*, written in 1643, Williams'
subject matter was diverse, from styles of lodging, to the making of
wampum, hunting and trading. The sections are titled: "of Mar-
riage", "Of the Sea", etc.

Grave of the Twelve-Year-Old Pequot Girl
This interesting story is recounted in the article: "The Trout and
The Milk: An Ethnobibliographical Talk" by Hugh Amory.

Snake, Fish, Stone
Based on the 1902 diary of Fidelia Fielding, as of the 1930s she
was considered the last fluent speaker of Mohegan-Pequot. "Native
Tribes and Dialects of Connecticut" by Frank Speck.

Narragansett Midwife's Testimony
Based, in part, on the story of Sarah Pharoah, a Narragansett woman accused of, and brought to trial for infanticide in 1730.

Out of Wedlock
The phrase *idea without hands* was a term spoken by Bronson Alcott to describe his wife Abigail. *My Heart is Boundless* by Eva LaPlante.

John Eliot Creates Indian Grammar
Some words in italics were taken from *A Grammar of the Massachusetts Indian Language 1822* by John Eliot

Judges
Phrases were taken and altered from marginalia in the bibles of Northeastern Indians, transcribed in *Native Writings in Massachusett* by Ives Goddard and Kathleen Bragdon.

Deer Island
During King Philip's War, Native Americans known to the settlers as 'praying Indians' because of their conversion to Christianity were rounded up and interred on Deer Island just outside Boston harbor. They remained on the island for the duration of the war where many died from starvation and exposure.

II

Loss
Some words in italics were spoken by Pretty-shield to Frank Linderman in the book *Pretty-shield Medicine Woman of the Crows* by Frank Linderman

Incantation To Affect Two Women
Some italicized lines were taken from *Walk in Your Soul: Love Incantations of the Oklahoma Cherokees* written by Jack Kilpatrick and Anna Gritts Kilpatrick.

Courtship scene drawn on an envelope
The actual drawing was done by an unknown Cheyenne artist. It is owned by the Southwest Museum of Los Angeles and appears in the book *Sending My Heart Back Across the Years* by Hertha Dawn Wong.

Doomed of Oklahoma
Nowhere to stretch your heart was the title of a Pima goodbye song.

Peculiar Confederacy
"My people are small; their shadow scarcely reaches to your knee; they are scattered and gone." Spoken in 1843 by Mississippi Choctaw Chief Cobb in a claim to the federal agent in charge of emigration. *After Removal: The Choctaw in Mississippi* edited by Samuel J Wells and Roseanna Tubby.

Another crow hangs
Words in italics were taken from the *Master Letters* by Emily Dickinson.

Deed of Gift
The story of the slave named Doll is recounted in the book-length study *Ties That Bind; The Story of an Afro-Cherokee Family in Slavery and Freedom* by Tiya Miles.

***Indian Exhibit;* The Trans-Mississippi and International Exhibition 1898**
This grass house and tipi and windbreak was spoken by the Ethnologist James Mooney, who was a consultant on the Indian exhibit, called the Indian Congress. Mooney claimed the Congress had "degenerated into a Wild West show."

All the World's a Fair by Robert W. Rydell

these once formidable enemies/of white man/camped together in a frame—was adapted from an article in the Omaha Bee in 1898 as it appeared in *All the World's a Fair* by Robert W. Rydell

The Lost People
Like a feather on a sore spot was spoken by John Fire Lame Deer. *The Sixth Grandfather* edited by Raymond De Mallie

The Pan-American Exhibition; Buffalo 1901
Behold, the world is a sucked orange is attributed to a journalist writing in reference to the Trip to the Moon exhibit at the Pan American Exhibition in 1901.

All the World's a Fair by Robert W. Rydell

Renaming at Boarding School
"The ridiculous and uncouth names that many of our Indian young people have is becoming embarrassing, and I am wondering if it is possible to consider changing some of these names to more modern names that will not, at least, be a handicap to the students."
James McGregor a district superintendent. *Boarding School Seasons* by Brenda Child

The Myth of Fish
They wanted to swim on their own. Some even avoided schools as much as possible was spoken by lead researcher Tomas Brodin, Umea University, Sweden, referring to the affects of anti anxiety drug Oxazepam on wild perch; as reported by Reuters.

I offer this to you who are down in the water with wings of red from Black Elk's teachings. *The Sixth Grandfather* edited by Raymond De Mallie

Acknowledgments

My thanks to the journals in which versions of the following poems have appeared or are forthcoming.

Apalachee Review: "Dear Reverend"

Cider Press Review: "Grave of the Twelve-Year-Old Pequot Girl"

The Massachusetts Review: "Trinket-Shine", "Her Moods Caused Owls"

Passages North: "Deed of Gift", "Sometimes They Keep a Horse"

Salt Hill Journal: "The Dead's Bright Copperas"

Tupelo Quarterly: "Removal (Treaty of Dancing Rabbit Creek)"

"The Art of Flying" first appeared in *The Comstock Review* and in the collection *Church of Needles* published by Red Mountain Press

About the Author

Sarah Sousa's poems have appeared or are forthcoming in *The Massachusetts Review, Passages North, Barn Owl Review, Cider Press Review* and *Salt Hill Journal* among others. She has been nominated for a Pushcart Prize. Her first collection *Church of Needles* won the Red Mountain Press Prize and was published in May 2014 by Red Mountain Press. She also edited and transcribed *The Diary of Esther Small; 1886*, published by Small Batch Books. Her poem "Learning My Name" is affixed to a stone pillar at Edmands Park in Newton, Massachusetts as part of the Poetry in the Park Project. She holds an MFA from Bennington College and lives in Western Massachusetts with her husband and two sons.

Photograph of the author by Tobias LaMontagne.
Used by permission.

Free Verse Editions

Edited by Jon Thompson

13 ways of happily by Emily Carr
Between the Twilight and the Sky by Jennie Neighbors
Blood Orbits by Ger Killeen
The Bodies by Chris Sindt
The Book of Isaac by Aidan Semmens
Canticle of the Night Path by Jennifer Atkinson
Child in the Road by Cindy Savett
Condominium of the Flesh by Valerio Magrelli, translated by Clarissa
    Botsford
Contrapuntal by Christopher Kondrich
Country Album by James Capozzi
The Curiosities by Brittany Perham
Current by Lisa Fishman
Dismantling the Angel by Eric Pankey
Divination Machine by F. Daniel Rzicznek
Erros by Morgan Lucas Schuldt
The Forever Notes by Ethel Rackin
The Flying House by Dawn-Michelle Baude
Instances: Selected Poems by Jeongrye Choi, translated by Brenda
    Hillman, Wayne de Fremery, & Jeongrye Choi
The Magnetic Brackets by Jesús Losada, translated by Michael Smith
    & Luis Ingelmo
A Map of Faring by Peter Riley
No Shape Bends the River So Long by Monica Berlin & Beth Marzoni
Pilgrimly by Siobhan Scarry
Physis by Nicolas Pesque, translated by Cole Swensen
Poems from above the Hill & Selected Work by Ashur Etwebi, translated
    by Brenda Hillman & Diallah Haidar
The Prison Poems by Miguel Hernández, translated by Michael Smith
Puppet Wardrobe by Daniel Tiffany
Quarry by Carolyn Guinzio
remanence by Boyer Rickel
Signs Following by Ger Killeen
Split the Crow by Sarah Sousa
Summoned by Guillevic, translated by Monique Chefdor
Sunshine Wound by L. S. Klatt

These Beautiful Limits by Thomas Lisk
An Unchanging Blue: Selected Poems 1962–1975 by Rolf Dieter
    Brinkmann, translated by Mark Terrill
Under the Quick by Molly Bendall
Verge by Morgan Lucas Schuldt
The Wash by Adam Clay
We'll See by George Godeau, translated by Kathleen McGookey
What Stillness Illuminated by Yermiyahu Ahron Taub
Winter Journey [Viaggio d'inverno] by Attilio Bertolucci, translated by
    Nicholas Benson
Wonder Rooms by Allison Funk

CPSIA information can be obtained
at www.ICGtesting.com
Printed in the USA
BVHW08s1338150618
519070BV00003B/192/P

9 781602 356351